Can You Read a Map?

Dining Room

Papa

Mama

Bedroom

Sitting Room

2 **Can you read the three bears' map?**

Village

Woodcutter's House

Woods

'Red's House

Grandma's House

To Another Fairy Tale

Can you read Little Red Riding Hood's map? 3

Hansel
and
Gretel's
House

Deep Dark Forest

Froggy Po

Lookout
Mountain

Witch's House

4   **Can you read Hansel and Gretel's map?**

Can you read Cinderella's map?

5

Can you read the Wolf's map?

Which way should he go?